Ad Libs for

A+ Hilarious Teachers

Fill-in-the-Blank Story Games

JBC Story Press

Copyright ©2022. All rights reserved.

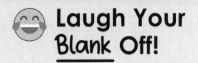

Laugh Your Blank Off!

Ad Libs for Adults
How to Play

Welcome! And get ready to laugh your blank off!

Number of players: 2-200+

There's really no limit… The more the merrier! This game is perfect for parties or just hanging out with friends. Players don't even have to be in the same room. Playing through video chat works great too.

Inside, you'll find 21 entertaining stories with blank spaces where words have been left out. Each story comes with a list of missing words of various types, e.g., ADJECTIVE, ADVERB, NOUN, EXCLAMATION, etc.

For each story, one player is the Story Teller. The Story Teller asks the other players to call out words to fill in the spaces of the story — WITHOUT first telling them what the story is about.

And bam! Just like that, you have a RIDICULOUSLY funny story!

The Story Teller reads the completed story out loud, and you all laugh so hard you almost pee your pants, cry, roll on the floor, or all of the above! *YOU* fill in the blank!

Adult Themes

This version of the game is for "grownups." That means stories may contain references to alcohol, romance, and other crazy adult stuff (you know, like work or parenting). Whether stories include "adult" language is up to you! Some groups like to use "salty" swear words. Others prefer "sweet" and swear-free. It's your call!

One thing's for sure. Every story you create will be RIDICULOUSLY funny!

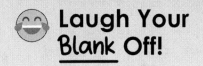

Laugh Your Blank Off!

Ad Libs for Adults
How to Play

Examples

Before, with blanks:

"_____! We need to _____ to the party as
　EXCLAMATION　　　　　　　　　VERB

_____ as possible. We only have _____ minutes to get
ADVERB ENDING IN "LY"　　　　　　　　　　　　NUMBER

there." So we jumped in the _____ car and sped off.
　　　　　　　　　　　　　　　　　ADJECTIVE

After the Story Teller fills in the blanks with words from the players:

"__Yuck__! We need to __dance__ to the party as
　EXCLAMATION　　　　　　　　VERB

__quietly__ as possible. We only have __900__ minutes to get
ADVERB ENDING IN "LY"　　　　　　　　　NUMBER

there." So we jumped in the __furry__ car and sped off.
　　　　　　　　　　　　　　　ADJECTIVE

Quick Review

ADJECTIVE – Describes something or someone. Examples: Funny, huge, bossy, lame, fast.

ADVERB – Describes how something is done. You will only be asked for adverbs that end in "ly." Examples: Happily, badly, loudly.

NOUN or PLURAL NOUN – A person, place or thing. Examples: Singular – sister, book, foot. Plural – sisters, books, feet.

VERB, VERB ENDING IN "ING" or VERB (PAST TENSE) – Verbs are action words. Examples: Verb – Run, kiss, sing; Verb ending in "ing"– running, kissing, singing; Verb (past tense) – ran, kissed, sang

EXCLAMATION – A sound, word, or phrase that is spoken suddenly or loudly and expresses emotions, like excitement or anger, or shock or pain. Examples: "Oh no!", "Awesome!", "You're kidding me!", "Oof!"

OTHER – Specific words, like ANIMAL, BODY PART, CITY, COLOR, FIRST NAME (FRIEND)

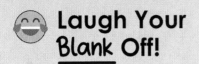

Laugh Your Blank Off!

Things Students Do That Drive Teachers Crazy

NUMBER
NOUN
ADVERB ENDING IN "LY"
ADJECTIVE
BODY PART
EXCLAMATION
VERB
NUMBER
NOUN
ADJECTIVE
NOUN
PLURAL NOUN
VERB
ADJECTIVE
BODY PART (PLURAL)
SILLY SOUND

From *Hilarious Teachers Ad Libs for Adults* ©2022, JBC Story Press

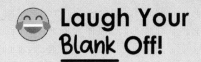

Laugh Your Blank Off!

Things Students Do That Drive Teachers Crazy

Honest question: Can you die from repeating instructions _____ (NUMBER) times an hour? Because it definitely feels possible. If I had a _____ (NOUN) for every time a student asked, "What are we supposed to be doing?", just moments after I _____ (ADVERB ENDING IN "LY") explained the instructions that are on the paper in front of them, written in _____ (ADJECTIVE) letters on the board, and practically printed on my _____ (BODY PART), I could afford to retire right now. _____ (EXCLAMATION)! I could afford to retire all the teachers at my school! Somehow, it gets even worse when students try to _____ (VERB) the instructions. For example: Me: "Please take out one sheet of paper, write your name in the upper left corner, and write _____ (NUMBER) sentences about your _____ (NOUN)." Them: "Our first and last name? Can we just write two _____ (ADJECTIVE) sentences? Should we use a pencil? Is this for a _____ (NOUN)?" It's like death by a thousand _____ (PLURAL NOUN)! Speaking of things that could _____ (VERB) you. Why do kids, including ones who are _____ (ADJECTIVE) enough to know better, put things in their _____ (BODY PART (PLURAL)) that are not food! And don't even get me started on _____ (SILLY SOUND)-Talk challenges. Serenity now!

From *Hilarious Teachers Ad Libs for Adults* ©2022, JBC Story Press

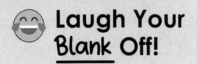

Laugh Your Blank Off!

Ice Breakers That Teachers Actually Love

ADJECTIVE
ADJECTIVE
BODY PART (PLURAL)
ADJECTIVE
PLURAL NOUN
NOUN
VERB (PAST TENSE)
EXCLAMATION
NUMBER
NOUN
PLURAL NOUN
ADJECTIVE
NOUN
NOUN
ADJECTIVE
COLOR
NUMBER

From *Hilarious Teachers Ad Libs for Adults* ©2022 JBC Story Press

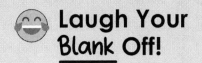

Laugh Your Blank Off!

Ice Breakers That Teachers Actually Love

Spoiler alert! There aren't any! Because, as you know from your own _____ (ADJECTIVE) experience, teachers despise icebreakers! Sure, there a few _____ (ADJECTIVE) teachers who think icebreakers are "kinda fun." But they're probably the same teachers who keep raising their _____ (BODY PART (PLURAL)) to ask questions and keep the meeting going. We asked _____ (ADJECTIVE) teachers about icebreakers and these _____ (PLURAL NOUN) sum it up:

- "We've been through _____ (NOUN) together. We already know each other. All the ice has been _____ (VERB (PAST TENSE)) into smithereens."

- "_____ (EXCLAMATION)! I have been teaching for _____ (NUMBER) years. I am done playing Human Bingo, Two Truths and a _____ (NOUN), and making _____ (PLURAL NOUN) out of toothpicks to bond with my equally _____ (ADJECTIVE) co-workers!"

- "Skip the _____ (NOUN) and let's get down to _____ (NOUN) so we can get back to doing _____ (ADJECTIVE) work."

- "We hate icebreakers with the _____ (COLOR)-hot intensity of _____ (NUMBER) suns."

Note to Admin: Skip the icebreaker! In fact, the whole meeting could just be an email!

From *Hilarious Teachers Ad Libs for Adults* ©2022, JBC Story Press

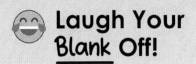

Laugh Your Blank Off!

Teachers Rock!

ADJECTIVE
ADJECTIVE
VERB
BODY PART
BODY PART (PLURAL)
VERB ENDING IN "ING"
VERB ENDING IN "ING"
VERB
VERB
CLOTHING ITEM (PLURAL)
PLURAL NOUN
VERB ENDING IN "ING"
NOUN
PLURAL NOUN
VERB
ADJECTIVE
ADJECTIVE
ADJECTIVE
VERB ENDING IN "ING"

From *Hilarious Teachers Ad Libs for Adults* ©2022, JBC Story Press

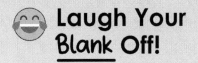

Laugh Your Blank Off!

Teachers Rock!

Being a teacher is awesome and *very* challenging. So it was nice when some _____ parents put up posters to decorate the
               ADJECTIVE

teacher's lounge. Here are some of the _____ quotes we
                                        ADJECTIVE

now see during the day: 1—Teach. Love. _____. 2—It
                                               VERB

takes a big _____ to shape little _____. 3—
           BODY PART   BODY PART (PLURAL)

Teachers who love _____ teach children who love
                 VERB ENDING IN "ING"

_____. 4—A truly great teacher is hard to _____,
VERB ENDING IN "ING"   VERB

difficult to part with and impossible to _____. 5—Not all
                                        VERB

superheroes wear _____, some have teaching degrees.
              CLOTHING ITEM (PLURAL)

6—Teachers plant _____ that grow forever. 7—
               PLURAL NOUN

_____ is heart work.
VERB ENDING IN "ING"

8—Never underestimate the _____ you make or the
                                NOUN

_____ you touch. 9—It takes a lot of sparkle to
PLURAL NOUN

_____ a teacher. 10—Keep _____ and pretend
  VERB   ADJECTIVE

it's on the lesson plan. 11—I'm a teacher. To save time, let's just

assume I'm always _____. 12—Being a teacher is
                  ADJECTIVE

_____. It's like _____ a bike. If the bike is on fire.
ADJECTIVE   VERB ENDING IN "ING"

You're on fire. Everything's on fire.

From *Hilarious Teachers Ad Libs for Adults* ©2022, JBC Story Press

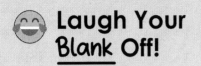

Laugh Your Blank Off!

Crazy Parent Types

ADJECTIVE
ADJECTIVE
VERB
BODY PART
NOUN
VERB ENDING IN "ING"
FIRST NAME (ANYONE)
ADJECTIVE
ADJECTIVE
ADJECTIVE
PLURAL NOUN
VERB
EXCLAMATION
ADJECTIVE
ADJECTIVE
NOUN
ADJECTIVE

From *Hilarious Teachers Ad Libs for Adults* ©2022 JBC Story Press

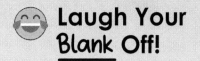

Laugh Your Blank Off!

Crazy Parent Types

Most parents are _____, but every teacher runs into a
                      ADJECTIVE

few bad apples during the year. Like these _____ parent
                                                    ADJECTIVE

types that every teacher encounters. 1—The "My Child Can

_____ No Wrong" Parent: How some parents can keep a
    VERB

straight _____ when they tell us that their kid is a little
             BODY PART

_____, 24/7, is mind-_____. They are either
    NOUN   VERB ENDING IN "ING"

_____-winning actors or totally _____. But we
FIRST NAME (ANYONE)   ADJECTIVE

know the truth! 2—The "You Don't Understand How

_____ My Child Is" Parent: Yes, your child is unique and
   ADJECTIVE

_____ and no, that doesn't mean they can choose which
   ADJECTIVE

assignments they want to do or _____ they want to
                                    PLURAL NOUN

follow. 3—The "You _____ Too Much Homework" Parent:
                          VERB

_____! We don't want to grade any more assignments
EXCLAMATION

than we have too! Maybe if they didn't do their kids homework for

them they wouldn't be so _____. 4—The "No-
                                ADJECTIVE

Boundaries" Parent: They send you _____ texts and
                                          ADJECTIVE

emails at all hours of the day. If you don't respond within minutes,

brace yourself for a phone call asking, "Did you get my

_____?" Dealing with these kinds of parents at school is
    NOUN

_____ enough. Here's hoping you don't run into them
  ADJECTIVE

around town as well!

From *Hilarious Teachers Ad Libs for Adults* ©2022, JBC Story Press

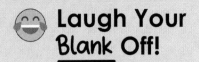

Laugh Your Blank Off!

Students Say the Darndest Things

OCCUPATION (PLURAL)
BODY PART (PLURAL)
PLURAL NOUN
VERB
NOUN
ADJECTIVE
BODY PART
COLOR
CLOTHING ITEM
ADJECTIVE
ANIMAL
LAST NAME (FRIEND)
RELATIVE (e.g., MOM, COUSIN)
VERB
ADJECTIVE
BODY PART (PLURAL)
RELATIVE (e.g., MOM, COUSIN)

From *Hilarious Teachers Ad Libs for Adults* ©2022, JBC Story Press

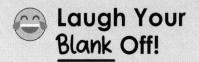

Laugh Your Blank Off!

Students Say the Darndest Things

Students are natural _____. You never know what
                        OCCUPATION (PLURAL)

comedy gems are going to come out of their _____. We
                                            BODY PART (PLURAL)

may be in the middle of teaching about _____ and
                                         PLURAL NOUN

someone will ask a question that makes everyone _____
                                                    VERB

out loud. Even when a student is trying to give us a nice

_____, it can come out a little _____. Here are
   NOUN   ADJECTIVE

some real-life examples from teachers:

- "I know why your _____ is so big…To hold your big
                      BODY PART

  heart!"

- "Commenting on my plaid _____ _____: 'You
                              COLOR   CLOTHING ITEM

  look like a really _____ scarecrow.'"
                        ADJECTIVE

- "A student gave me a note that said, 'You are prettier than a(n)

  _____.'"
      ANIMAL

- "I love you, Ms. _____! My _____ doesn't
                   LAST NAME (FRIEND)   RELATIVE

  _____ you, but I love you!"
      VERB

- "With your hair you look like a(n) _____ witch from the
                                        ADJECTIVE

  woods. But a nice one."

- "You remind me of my mom!" Me: "Really? Why is that?"

  "Because my mom's _____ sag!"
                     BODY PART (PLURAL)

As one teacher said, "The biggest compliment is when they call

me _____!" We couldn't agree more!
     RELATIVE

From *Hilarious Teachers Ad Libs for Adults* ©2022, JBC Story Press

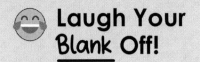 # Laugh Your Blank Off!

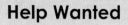 **Help Wanted**

NOUN
ADJECTIVE
VERB ENDING IN "ING"
VERB
OCCUPATION (PLURAL)
VERB
ADJECTIVE
ADJECTIVE
VERB ENDING IN "ING"
PLURAL NOUN
BODY PART
NUMBER
NOUN
VERB ENDING IN "ING"
BODY PART
PLURAL NOUN
NOUN
PLURAL NOUN

From *Hilarious Teachers Ad Libs for Adults* ©2022 JBC Story Press

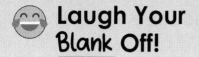

Laugh Your Blank Off!

Help Wanted

_____-ville Elementary School is looking for a fifth grade
    NOUN

teacher to start immediately. _____ applicants will have:
                                   ADJECTIVE

1—A bachelor's or master's degree and _____ certificate.
                                          VERB ENDING IN "ING"

2—The ability to _____ through ever-changing hoops
                       VERB

created by _____ to do your job. 3—The ability to
            OCCUPATION (PLURAL)

_____ lesson plans without any prep time. 4—
     VERB

_____ communication skills for dealing with
   ADJECTIVE

_____ students and parents. 5—A commitment to
   ADJECTIVE

_____ in daily staff meetings, including asking lots of
VERB ENDING IN "ING"

_____. 6—A huge _____ capable of holding
 PLURAL NOUN   BODY PART

_____ cups of coffee between rare bathroom breaks. 7—Other
 NUMBER

duties will be assigned, with no extra pay, of course, like

_____ duty or _____ at school events. Paying
    NOUN   VERB ENDING IN "ING"

for school supplies, like _____ sanitizer, _____,
                            BODY PART   PLURAL NOUN

and educational _____ decorations is not required, but
                    NOUN

still expected. As a top school district, our _____ are very
                                                PLURAL NOUN

high—unlike the salaries we pay. You do not have to be crazy to

work here. We will train you!

From *Hilarious Teachers Ad Libs for Adults* ©2022, JBC Story Press

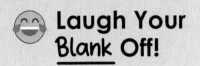

Laugh Your Blank Off!

Too Much Free Time

VERB
VERB ENDING IN "ING"
ADJECTIVE
VERB ENDING IN "ING"
PLURAL NOUN
VERB ENDING IN "ING"
ADVERB ENDING IN "LY"
VERB ENDING IN "ING"
VERB ENDING IN "ING"
PLURAL NOUN
ADJECTIVE
ADJECTIVE
ADJECTIVE
VERB
TV SHOW
EXCLAMATION
NOUN

From *Hilarious Teachers Ad Libs for Adults* ©2022 JBC Story Press

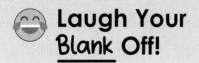

Laugh Your Blank Off!

Too Much Free Time

As everyone knows, one of the biggest problems teachers

_____ today is having too much free time. And by "free
　　VERB

time," we mean *unpaid* time _____ unrealistic work
　　　　　　　　　　　　　　　VERB ENDING IN "ING"

demands! Which gives us loads of time for _____ teacher
　　　　　　　　　　　　　　　　　　　　　ADJECTIVE

"hobbies," like:

- _____ in our cars.
  VERB ENDING IN "ING"
- Grading stacks of _____.
  　　　　　　　　　PLURAL NOUN
- _____ the bathroom whenever we want.
  VERB ENDING IN "ING"
- Building (and _____ drinking) our wine collection.
  　　　　　　ADVERB ENDING IN "LY"
- _____ asleep by 7 p.m. on a Friday night.
  VERB ENDING IN "ING"
- _____ for school supplies that schools don't supply.
  VERB ENDING IN "ING"
- Making crafts, like _____ that resemble
  　　　　　　　　　PLURAL NOUN
  _____ parents and sticking pins in them.
  ADJECTIVE
- Learning magic tricks, like how to pay _____ bills with
  　　　　　　　　　　　　　　　　　　　ADJECTIVE
  a(n) _____ paycheck.
  　　　ADJECTIVE
- _____-watching reruns of _____ while
  VERB　　　　　　　　　　　　　**TV SHOW**
  ignoring the "Sunday Scaries."

_____! Time sure flies when you're having
EXCLAMATION

_____!
NOUN

From *Hilarious Teachers Ad Libs for Adults* ©2022, JBC Story Press

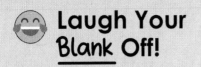

Laugh Your Blank Off!

Awkward Encounters

VERB ENDING IN "ING"
NOUN
ADJECTIVE
BEVERAGE
BODY PART
EXCLAMATION
ADJECTIVE
TYPE OF BUSINESS
CLOTHING ITEM
NOUN
ADVERB ENDING IN "LY"
ADJECTIVE
NUMBER
LAST NAME (FRIEND)
NOUN
VERB

From *Hilarious Teachers Ad Libs for Adults* ©2022 JBC Story Press

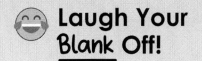

Laugh Your Blank Off!   Awkward Encounters

_____ parents and students in public is just part of
VERB ENDING IN "ING"

teacher life. It's not always awkward. Students, especially young

ones, can make you feel like a _____ star when they see
NOUN

you outside of school. But these encounters can be very

_____. Here are some examples teachers shared: 1—At
ADJECTIVE

the liquor store: "There was a great sale of my favorite

_____, so I was buying cases to get me through the
BEVERAGE

school year — or at least the month (Ha!) — when I felt a tap on

my _____. It was my school's PTA President.
BODY PART

'_____! Are you having a party?', she asked. I was so
EXCLAMATION

_____." 2—At an all-night _____: "It was very
ADJECTIVE   TYPE OF BUSINESS

late and I was in my comfy clothes, _____-less, of
CLOTHING ITEM

course, scanning the shelves for _____ relief.
NOUN

_____, one of my student's moms appears and tries to
ADVERB ENDING IN "LY"

hold a parent conference with me." 3—On vacation: "I try to go as

far away as possible! So, I was _____ when I heard a
ADJECTIVE

familiar shriek outside the beach house my friends and I had

rented _____ hours away from home. 'Hi Ms. _____!
NUMBER   LAST NAME (FRIEND)

What are you doing here?!' That's right, my most challenging

student and his _____ were staying right next door." You
NOUN

just can't _____ this stuff up!
VERB

From *Hilarious Teachers Ad Libs for Adults* ©2022, JBC Story Press

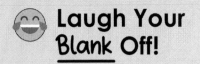

Laugh Your Blank Off!

Extreme Sidehustle

FIRST & LAST NAME (FRIEND)
ADJECTIVE
TYPE OF BUSINESS
NOUN
ADJECTIVE
CLOTHING ITEM
BODY PART
BODY PART (PLURAL)
BODY PART (PLURAL)
BODY PART (PLURAL)
EXCLAMATION
VERB (PAST TENSE)
NUMBER
NOUN
GRADE LEVEL
CITY
PLURAL NOUN

From *Hilarious Teachers Ad Libs for Adults* ©2022 JBC Story Press

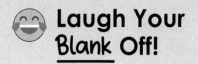 # Laugh Your Blank Off!

Extreme Sidehustle

This is _____, with YNN, bringing you a(n)
    FIRST & LAST NAME (FRIEND)

_____ report about an attempted robbery. Police say that
   ADJECTIVE

the suspect entered a local _____ just before closing and
                                       TYPE OF BUSINESS

demanded _____. According to witnesses, the suspect
                NOUN

burst in wearing a(n) _____ _____ over her
                         ADJECTIVE   CLOTHING ITEM

_____. She yelled, "Attention friends! _____ on
 BODY PART   BODY PART (PLURAL)

me! I want a straight line next to the wall. Keep your

_____ to yourselves your _____ closed." When
BODY PART (PLURAL)   BODY PART (PLURAL)

asked if she was armed, one witness said, "_____! Who
                                                            EXCLAMATION

knows? She had such a commanding voice that we just did what

she said." Police _____ the suspect in the parking lot
                     VERB (PAST TENSE)

when her _____-year old getaway _____ wouldn't
         NUMBER   NOUN

start. As if this incident wasn't shocking enough, authorities

confirmed that the suspect is a _____ teacher from
                                    GRADE LEVEL

_____School District. As she was led away in
   CITY

_____, an onlooker shouted, "Crime doesn't pay!" And
PLURAL NOUN

the suspect shouted back, "Neither does teaching!"

From Hilarious Teachers Ad Libs for Adults ©2022, JBC Story Press

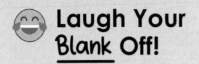

Laugh Your Blank Off!

When Admin Finally Listens to You

LAST NAME (ANYONE)
VERB ENDING IN "ING"
ADJECTIVE
ADJECTIVE
VERB
VERB
ADJECTIVE
VERB ENDING IN "ING"
ADJECTIVE
NOUN
ADVERB ENDING IN "LY"
VERB ENDING IN "ING"
VERB ENDING IN "ING"

From *Hilarious Teachers Ad Libs for Adults* ©2022 JBC Story Press

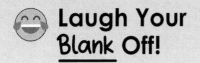

Laugh Your Blank Off!

When Admin Finally Listens to You

TO: All School Staff

FROM: Principal _____-burger
                    LAST NAME (ANYONE)

Thank you for _____ our Staff Survey. First, let me say
                VERB ENDING IN "ING"

that I heard you _____ and clear! So, I'm pleased to
                      ADJECTIVE

announce _____ policies to address your concerns: 1)
              ADJECTIVE

Better compensation - We can't pay you what you're worth

(because you're priceless!), but you may now _____
                                                        VERB

jeans any day you want! Not just Fridays! And you no longer have

to _____ for the privilege. You may even wear them at
        VERB

home! 2) Low morale - Teaching is _____ work. But that
                                          ADJECTIVE

doesn't mean we can't have more fun doing it. So, we'll be

_____ more ice breakers than ever at staff meetings!
VERB ENDING IN "ING"

With _____ ice breakers, the fun never ends. Kind of like
          ADJECTIVE

our staff meetings! 3) Lack of support from administration - Your

_____ is my command! To give you the support you
    NOUN

_____ need, we will now have staff meetings every day.
ADVERB ENDING IN "LY"

That means even more ice breakers and fun! To make time for

mandatory meetings, lunch and _____ periods are now
                                      VERB ENDING IN "ING"

optional. Being prepared is still expected, of course, kind of like

_____ papers at home. The meetings will continue until
VERB ENDING IN "ING"

morale improves!

From *Hilarious Teachers Ad Libs for Adults* ©2022, JBC Story Press

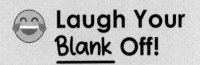

Laugh Your Blank Off!

Too Cool for School

LAST NAME (FRIEND)
ADJECTIVE
ADJECTIVE
VERB ENDING IN "ING"
COUNTRY
ADJECTIVE
NOUN
VERB
SPORT
NOUN
ADJECTIVE
VERB
PLURAL NOUN
VERB
ADJECTIVE
VERB
NOUN

From *Hilarious Teachers Ad Libs for Adults* ©2022, JBC Story Press

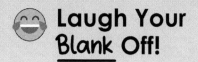

Laugh Your Blank Off!

Too Cool for School

Hey Ms. _____! Hope you're having a(n) _____
　　　　　LAST NAME (FRIEND)　　　　　　　　　　　　　　　　　　ADJECTIVE

day!!! I've been so crazy _____ _____ and
　　　　　　　　　　　　　　ADJECTIVE　　VERB ENDING IN "ING"

packing that I almost forgot to tell you! Tomorrow, we leave for our

vacation in _____, so Brad won't be in class this week.
　　　　　　　COUNTRY

Will he miss anything important? You know what _____
　　　　　　　　　　　　　　　　　　　　　　　　　　　　ADJECTIVE

travel is like! We really need the extra _____, so we
　　　　　　　　　　　　　　　　　　　　　NOUN

figured, why not leave the week before school vacation? Schools

don't _____ much that week anyway, right? He'll get
　　　　VERB

caught up when he gets back. Of course, _____ season
　　　　　　　　　　　　　　　　　　　　　SPORT

is starting, so he'll have _____ after school, but he can
　　　　　　　　　　　　　NOUN

spread out his make-up work, right? As long as he gets the

_____ stuff done. We just want to _____ what
ADJECTIVE　　　　　　　　　　　　　　　　　　VERB

happened last year when his teacher gave him zeros for some

_____ he didn't do! He can just _____ the busy
PLURAL NOUN　　　　　　　　　　　　　　　　VERB

work, right? School is SOOOOO important, of course. But we just

can't pass up another chance to make _____ memories.
　　　　　　　　　　　　　　　　　　　　ADJECTIVE

And we'll share pics! You _____ our family on Instagram,
　　　　　　　　　　　　　VERB

right? Thanks in advance for making sure he doesn't fall behind in

_____!
NOUN

From *Hilarious Teachers Ad Libs for Adults* ©2022, JBC Story Press

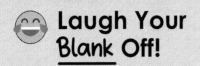

Laugh Your Blank Off!

Funny Teacher Fails

ADJECTIVE
VERB ENDING IN "ING"
ADJECTIVE
NOUN
ANIMAL
VERB ENDING IN "ING"
NOUN
VERB ENDING IN "ING"
CLOTHING ITEM (PLURAL)
ANIMAL (PLURAL NOUN)
VERB (PAST TENSE)
ADJECTIVE
BODY PART
VERB ENDING IN "ING"

From *Hilarious Teachers Ad Libs for Adults* ©2022, JBC Story Press

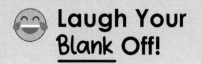

Laugh Your Blank Off!

Funny Teacher Fails

We've all made _____ mistakes at school. At the risk of
                          ADJECTIVE

_____ cringe attacks for some of you, check out these
VERB ENDING IN "ING"

_____ "fails" that teachers shared:
ADJECTIVE

- "Used a _____ stick on my lips by mistake."
              NOUN

- "Had to tell my class, 'Sorry, my _____ ate your
                                      ANIMAL
  homework.'"

- "My fifth graders were _____ basketballs during
                          VERB ENDING IN "ING"

  _____ and I needed to make an announcement.
  NOUN

  Without _____, I yelled 'Everyone hold your balls!'"
           VERB ENDING IN "ING"

- "I wore mismatched _____ and socks!"
                      CLOTHING ITEM (PLURAL)

- "I bought two male _____ as class pets. Turns out,
                      ANIMAL (PLURAL NOUN)

  they weren't both male. We _____ a LOT of class
                              VERB (PAST TENSE)

  pets that year."

- "For the first field trip that I supervised, I was so

  _____ when I did the final _____-count on
  ADJECTIVE   BODY PART

  the bus before returning to school. We had the same number

  of students that we came with! I was _____ myself on
                                         VERB ENDING IN "ING"

  the back when I realized one of the kids on the bus wasn't

  from our school!"

Live and learn! And laugh a lot too, of course.

From Hilarious Teachers Ad Libs for Adults ©2022, JBC Story Press

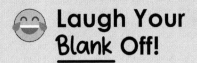

Laugh Your Blank Off!

Fixing the Teacher Sub Shortage

VERB
ADJECTIVE
EXCLAMATION
STATE
ADJECTIVE
ADJECTIVE
VERB ENDING IN "ING"
VERB
NOUN
FOOD
EXCLAMATION
ADJECTIVE
ADJECTIVE
NOUN
EMOTION

From *Hilarious Teachers Ad Libs for Adults* ©2022, JBC Story Press

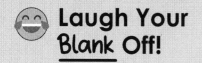

Laugh Your Blank Off!

Fixing the Teacher Sub Shortage

Host: "Welcome Commissioner _____-face. Thank you
                                        VERB

for joining us today on the _____ Educator Podcast."
                                    ADJECTIVE

Guest: "Thanks for having me! I'm a big fan of the show."

Host: "_____! Let's get right to our topic, then. Schools in
        EXCLAMATION

your state of _____ and across the country are struggling
                    STATE

with a(n) _____ shortage of substitute teachers. But
            ADJECTIVE

you've come up with a(n) _____ solution, right?"
                                ADJECTIVE

Guest: "That's right. When we realized that teachers were going to

keep needing basic things, like sick days, or would keep

_____ due to unrealistic demands and poor pay, we knew
VERB ENDING IN "ING"

we needed to _____ outside the _____. And
                    VERB   NOUN

then it hit me one day when I was ordering delivery of my favorite

_____ sub for lunch. We should partner with Uber for
    FOOD

teacher subs!"

Host: "_____! So you're hiring Uber drivers as subs? Are
        EXCLAMATION

they qualified?"

Guest: "Of course! If by 'qualified' you mean they're a(n)

_____ body we can park behind a desk to supervise a
    ADJECTIVE

class of _____ kids. And we only hire drivers who
            ADJECTIVE

average at least a 2-star _____."
                                NOUN

Host: "Nice! I'm sure parents will be _____ to hear that."
                                            EMOTION

From *Hilarious Teachers Ad Libs for Adults* ©2022, JBC Story Press

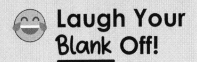

Laugh Your Blank Off!

Diplomatic Teacher Talk

ADJECTIVE
ADJECTIVE
PLURAL NOUN
VERB ENDING IN "ING"
PLURAL NOUN
VERB
NOUN
NOUN
VERB
NOUN
NOUN
VERB
VERB

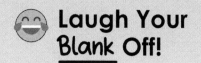

Laugh Your Blank Off!

Diplomatic Teacher Talk

Teachers are _____ communicators and parent-teacher
                    ADJECTIVE

conferences are the _____ test of those skills. Here are
                         ADJECTIVE

examples of diplomatic _____ that we use when
                            PLURAL NOUN

describing students to their parents: 1—When we say: "He is very

social!" We mean: "He will not stop _____ during class."
                                     VERB ENDING IN "ING"

2—When we say: "She is very concerned about her

_____." We mean: "She tattles on everyone non-stop."
PLURAL NOUN

3—When we say: "I would like to _____ more
                                       VERB

independence in your son." We mean: "Please stop doing his

_____ for him." 4—When we say: "She has
NOUN

_____ skills" We mean: "She is very bossy." 5—When we
NOUN

say: "I am envious of his energy!" We mean: "Do you

_____ him a whole _____ of sugar in the
VERB   NOUN

morning or mix in a little cereal?" 6—When we say: "I think she is

going to be a teacher when she grows up." We mean: "She tries to

tell me how to do my _____ every day." 7—When we say:
                          NOUN

"He has told me so much about you!" We mean: "I won't

_____ everything he says about you if you won't
VERB

_____ everything he says about me."
VERB

From *Hilarious Teachers Ad Libs for Adults* ©2022, JBC Story Press

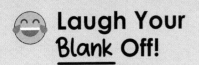

Laugh Your Blank Off!

Swear Like a Teacher

EXCLAMATION
FIRST NAME (FRIEND 1)
EXCLAMATION
FIRST NAME (FRIEND 2)
NOUN
NOUN THAT BEGINS WITH "S"
ADJECTIVE
ADJECTIVE
ADJECTIVE
VERB THAT BEGINS WITH "F"
ANIMAL
NOUN THAT BEGINS WITH "S"
VERB THAT BEGINS WITH "F"
NOUN THAT BEGINS WITH "H"
ADJECTIVE
VERB THAT BEGINS WITH "F"
ADJECTIVE

From *Hilarious Teachers Ad Libs for Adults* ©2022 JBC Story Press

Laugh Your Blank Off!

Swear Like a Teacher

"_____!," said _____. "I said '_____!' in
  EXCLAMATION   FIRST NAME (FRIEND 1)   EXCLAMATION

front of my kids again." "Been there, done that!" said

_____. "And you know your little _____ will be
FIRST NAME (FRIEND 2)   NOUN

headline news when they get home. But, hey, _____
                                              NOUN THAT BEGINS WITH "S"

happens, right? So, I'm making a list of 'clean' swear words that

are _____ for the classroom. For example:
    ADJECTIVE

- Get another _____ email from a(n) _____
                  ADJECTIVE   ADJECTIVE

  parent? You can say, '_____ this!'
                    VERB THAT BEGINS WITH "F"

- Find out that the curriculum is changing again? You can say

  'That's total _____ _____!'
                ANIMAL   NOUN THAT BEGINS WITH "S"

- Hear that it will be indoor recess even though it's barely

  sprinkling ouside? You can say, 'What the _____?!'
                                      VERB THAT BEGINS WITH "F"

- If a student tells you that his mom let him come to school

  because he 'only threw up a little,' you can say: 'Oh,

  _____ no!'
  NOUN THAT BEGINS WITH "H"

- Did your _____ computer eat your lesson plans? You
          ADJECTIVE

  can say '_____ my life!'
    VERB THAT BEGINS WITH "F"

See? We can use _____ language that won't get us
                      ADJECTIVE

called to the Principal's office. We just have to get creative!"

From *Hilarious Teachers Ad Libs for Adults* ©2022, JBC Story Press

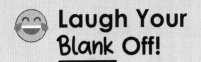 **Laugh Your Blank Off!**

Pop Quiz

ADJECTIVE
VERB ENDING IN "ING"
VERB ENDING IN "ING"
NUMBER
PLURAL NOUN
VERB
PLURAL NOUN
ADJECTIVE
NOUN
NOUN
VERB
ADJECTIVE
ADJECTIVE
VERB ENDING IN "ING"

From *Hilarious Teachers Ad Libs for Adults* ©2022 JBC Story Press

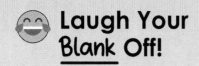

Laugh Your Blank Off!

Pop Quiz

It's pop quiz time, teachers! The _____ kind that you
                                        ADJECTIVE
don't have to study for or grade! True or False?

1. There are no stupid questions. False: Every question from "that teacher" that keeps the staff meeting _____ is a stupid
                                                         VERB ENDING IN "ING"
question. And every "What are we supposed to be

_____?" after you covered the instructions _____ times
VERB ENDING IN "ING"   NUMBER
is too.

2. Teachers don't have favorites. False: Of course we do! We love

all our _____, but there's always at least one who is not
         PLURAL NOUN
driving us to _____.
                VERB

3. Teachers are always honest with _____.
                                    PLURAL NOUN
True-ish: Sometimes we talk in code. When we say things like,

"He is a(n) _____ leader," we mean "He is always setting
             ADJECTIVE
a terrible example for classmates." But when we say we "love

having your child in my _____" we truly mean it!
                         NOUN

4. We love teaching. True! It's all the _____ that makes it
                                          NOUN
hard to teach that we _____. Things like a(n)
                        VERB

_____ workload, standardized tests, _____
 ADJECTIVE   ADJECTIVE
parents (not all of them, of course!), and micro-_____
                                                  VERB ENDING IN "ING"
bureaucrats. Great work on this quiz! Please reward yourself with

some chocolate, or a nice nap!

From *Hilarious Teachers Ad Libs for Adults* ©2022, JBC Story Press

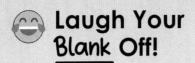 **Laugh Your Blank Off!**

Copier from Hell

VERB
ADJECTIVE
VERB
NOUN
VERB
LAST NAME (PRINCIPAL YOU KNOW)
ADJECTIVE
NOUN
VERB (PAST TENSE)
ADJECTIVE
VERB
PLURAL NOUN
ADJECTIVE
ANIMAL
ADJECTIVE
PLURAL NOUN
VERB ENDING IN "ING"
NOUN

From *Hilarious Teachers Ad Libs for Adults* ©2022, JBC Story Press

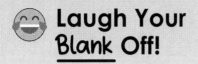

Laugh Your Blank Off!

Copier from Hell

"I hate to _____ our icebreaker, but I've invited a special
           VERB

guest to our staff meeting. As you know, our _____
                                                ADJECTIVE

copiers have a mind of their own. They won't _____
                                                   VERB

commands and keep jamming all day long! If you've seen him on

_____-Tube, you know our guest can _____.
    NOUN   VERB

Please welcome, The Copier Whisperer!" "Thank you for inviting

me, Principal _____. Teaching is _____ enough
              LAST NAME (PRINCIPAL YOU KNOW)   ADJECTIVE

without fighting with _____-shredding machines, so I'm
                           NOUN

happy to help. First, copiers don't like having their buttons

_____ any more than we do. So be gentle. You have a(n)
VERB (PAST TENSE)

_____ job, but try not to take it out on the copier or you
  ADJECTIVE

can _____ your precious papers goodbye. Second,
         VERB

copiers respond well to praise and _____. You might feel
                                      PLURAL NOUN

_____ at first, but whispering "Good work!" will keep the
  ADJECTIVE

copier purring like a(n) _____. And be sure to reward it
                            ANIMAL

with some nice _____ paper. Third, if the copier jams, DO
                  ADJECTIVE

NOT RUN! You can't outrun angry _____ who have to
                                    PLURAL NOUN

deal with your jam. Try _____ soothingly as you clear the
                        VERB ENDING IN "ING"

jam. If that doesn't work, don't panic. Just call us for service!

Breaking in a copier takes time, but with a little _____,
                                                        NOUN

you'll soon have a machine that doesn't eat your homework.

From *Hilarious Teachers Ad Libs for Adults* ©2022, JBC Story Press

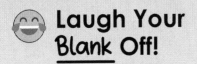

Laugh Your Blank Off!

Would You Rather for Teachers

| NOUN |
| BEVERAGE |
| VERB ENDING IN "ING" |
| VERB |
| VERB |
| ADJECTIVE |
| NOUN |
| VERB |
| NUMBER |
| VERB |
| PLURAL NOUN |
| NOUN |
| FOOD |
| VERB ENDING IN "ING" |
| VERB ENDING IN "ING" |
| PLURAL NOUN |

From *Hilarious Teachers Ad Libs for Adults* ©2022, JBC Story Press

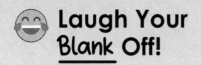

Laugh Your Blank Off!

Would You Rather for Teachers

Why should we let the kids have all the _____? Let's play
                                          NOUN
Would You Rather!

- Would you rather have a bottomless cup of _____
                                              BEVERAGE
  that's always the perfect temperature for _____ or be
                                              VERB ENDING IN "ING"
  able to _____ the restroom whenever you want?
          VERB

- If you could make someone _____ out of town by
                              VERB
  waving a(n) _____ wand, would you rather use it on a
               ADJECTIVE
  student or a _____?
                NOUN

- Would you rather _____ staff meetings every day or
                    VERB
  run into "that parent" every night.

- Would you rather have _____ straight days of indoor recess
                         NUMBER
  or one less day of school?

- Would you rather _____ a field trip or have an extra
                    VERB
  night of parent-teacher _____?
                           PLURAL NOUN

- Would you rather have a snack _____ filled with
                                  NOUN
  chocolate or with _____?
                     FOOD

- Would you rather hear that you'll be _____ a new
                                         VERB ENDING IN "ING"
  curriculum next year or _____ with a new Principal?
                           VERB ENDING IN "ING"

- Would you rather have a year's supply of Flair _____
                                                   PLURAL NOUN
  or a month without any copier jams?

From *Hilarious Teachers Ad Libs for Adults* ©2022, JBC Story Press

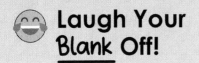

Laugh Your Blank Off!

Most Wished for Teacher Gifts

| NOUN |
| ADJECTIVE |
| NOUN |
| TYPE OF BUSINESS |
| TYPE OF BUSINESS |
| ADJECTIVE |
| PLURAL NOUN |
| EXCLAMATION |
| NUMBER |
| ADJECTIVE |
| VERB |
| FOOD |
| FOOD |
| VERB |
| BEVERAGE |
| NUMBER |
| VERB ENDING IN "ING" |
| ADJECTIVE |
| ADJECTIVE |

From *Hilarious Teachers Ad Libs for Adults* ©2022 JBC Story Press

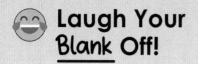# Laugh Your Blank Off!

Most Wished for Teacher Gifts

Looking for a holiday gift or a thank you _____ for
                                            NOUN
Teacher Appreciation Week? Every year, we ask teachers about

_____ gifts for teachers. If you guessed that gift cards top
ADJECTIVE

the _____, give yourself an A+! Check out some of their
      NOUN

most-wished for items:

- Gift cards: Pick one from a popular _____ or
                                       TYPE OF BUSINESS

  _____ and pop it into a(n) _____ gift card
  TYPE OF BUSINESS   ADJECTIVE
  holder to make it extra special!

- Tote bags: Perfect for carrying all those _____
                                              PLURAL NOUN
  teachers have to grade! _____! You might want to get
                           EXCLAMATION
  them _____! And we love the ones with _____ quotes
        NUMBER   ADJECTIVE
  on them, like "Teachers _____!"
                           VERB

- _____ Lovers Gift Basket: Every teacher needs a
  FOOD
  stash of _____ and other treats to help
            FOOD
  _____ them through the day.
  VERB

- _____ Mug Warmer: Let's face it! They probably own
  BEVERAGE
  _____ mugs by now! But what about a warmer to keep their
  NUMBER
  drink at the perfect temp for _____?
                                 VERB ENDING IN "ING"

The best part of any gift, of course, is a(n) _____ "Thank
                                                ADJECTIVE
You" note. Keeping it short and _____ works great!
                                  ADJECTIVE

From *Hilarious Teachers Ad Libs for Adults* ©2022, JBC Story Press

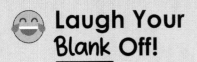

Laugh Your Blank Off!

Teachers vs. Students

| SPORT |
| PLURAL NOUN |
| COLOR |
| ANIMAL (PLURAL) |
| COLOR |
| PLURAL NOUN |
| NUMBER |
| VERB ENDING IN "ING" |
| ADJECTIVE |
| PLURAL NOUN |
| FOOD |
| NOUN |
| BODY PART |
| FOOD |
| LAST NAME (FRIEND) |
| ADJECTIVE |
| NOUN |
| ADJECTIVE |
| NUMBER |
| NOUN |

From *Hilarious Teachers Ad Libs for Adults* ©2022, JBC Story Press

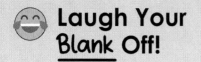

Teachers vs. Students

Please join us today for our annual Teachers vs. Students
_____ Game! It's a win-win! Everyone has fun and we
    SPORT
raise money for new _____ for the library. The students
                                   PLURAL NOUN
team is the _____ _____ and the teacher's team
                  COLOR   ANIMAL (PLURAL)
is the _____ _____. The teachers are trying to
          COLOR   PLURAL NOUN
break their _____-game losing streak, and the stakes are sky-
          NUMBER
high again this year: the winning team gets _____ rights
                                               VERB ENDING IN "ING"
and the losers have to wear _____ _____ for a
                             ADJECTIVE   PLURAL NOUN
whole school day. Parent volunteers will be selling grilled
_____, the 5th grade class is hosting a _____
   FOOD   NOUN
sale, and the art teacher will be offering _____-painting.
                                              BODY PART
There will also be a _____-eating contest where Principal
                       FOOD
_____ will try to repeat as champion. Be sure to buy lots
LAST NAME (FRIEND)
of raffle tickets! The grand prize is a(n) _____
                                            ADJECTIVE
_____! This _____ event starts at 4:00 p.m. and
  NOUN   ADJECTIVE
tickets are _____ dollars at the door. All proceeds go to a great
          NUMBER
_____, of course! Good luck to both teams!
  NOUN

From *Hilarious Teachers Ad Libs for Adults* ©2022, JBC Story Press

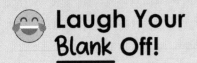

Laugh Your Blank Off!

Last Chance for Lost and Found

NOUN
NOUN
PLURAL NOUN
CLOTHING ITEM
VERB ENDING IN "ING"
CLOTHING ITEM (PLURAL)
PLURAL NOUN
PLURAL NOUN
NUMBER
ADJECTIVE
ADJECTIVE
CITY
COLOR
NOUN
ADJECTIVE
NUMBER
VERB (PAST TENSE)
NOUN
LAST NAME (FRIEND)

From *Hilarious Teachers Ad Libs for Adults* ©2022 JBC Story Press

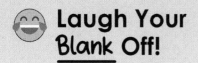

Laugh Your Blank Off!

Last Chance for Lost and Found

Dear _____ School Families,
      NOUN

Is your student missing a _____, _____, or a
                                    NOUN   PLURAL NOUN

_____? Please check the lost and found ASAP! The end
CLOTHING ITEM

of the school year is coming up fast, and our Lost-and-Found bins

are _____ with items. There are _____,
    VERB ENDING IN "ING"   CLOTHING ITEM (PLURAL)

_____, _____, _____ water bottles, eyeglasses,
PLURAL NOUN   PLURAL NOUN   NUMBER

and even some _____ retainers. Just a reminder that,
                 ADJECTIVE

after the _____ incident last year, when the
        ADJECTIVE

_____ HAZMAT team had to remove lunch bags covered
CITY

in toxic _____ _____, unclaimed lunch items are
      COLOR   NOUN

now thrown out daily. You know your _____ kid is going to
                                      ADJECTIVE

lose about _____ things during the school year, so please, put
        NUMBER

their name on all their things, so you can be notified. All items not

_____ by the last day of school will be either be donated
VERB (PAST TENSE)

to charity or thrown in the _____.
                            NOUN

Sincerely,

Principal _____
       LAST NAME (FRIEND)

From *Hilarious Teachers Ad Libs for Adults* ©2022, JBC Story Press

Thank you for trying us out

A favor please ♥

Would you take a quick minute to leave us a rating/review on Amazon? It makes a *HUGE* difference and we would really appreciate it!

More fun from JBC Story Press

To see more, visit this link
http://amazon.com/author/jbcstory or scan the QR code!

Do you like freebies?
Please send email to
info@jbcempowerpress.com
and we'll send you free funny stuff!

Made in United States
Orlando, FL
09 December 2024